THE POWER OF CRYSTAL HEALING

EMMA LUCY KNOWLES

STERLING ETHOS
New York

CONTENTS

Life is powerful
but so are you

When you harness, change, charge, heal and transform your energy you can change your life. This is an amazing gift. Feeling powerful in yourself is possible for everyone and much more achievable with a little help from some crystal sets.

We don't ever have to go through life, adventure, heartbreak, work, fear or fun on our own, but we can go through it at our own pace. We can do it loudly or we can do it in silence. And, most importantly, we can harness our own personal magic and allow ourselves to be enlarged, amplified and empowered by the hidden treasures held within nature's gems – better known to you and me as crystals.

Crystals are the ultimate powerhouses of the Earth, ready to raise your vibrations and share their healing properties – to walk with you, explore with you and teach you, to help you to develop your intuition and deepen your connection with yourself and your own personal energy.

Crystals are forever

Crystals are naturally occurring minerals with a unique crystal structure, formed under pressure over millions of years.

Crystals have been gracefully adorning our necks, rings, goblets and temples for years, decades and generations. They were a fond favorite of the Egyptians who turned the reflective magic of the hematite crystal into mirrors; the Greeks used to rub the same stone on their soldiers' bodies before they charged into battle. The Romans instinctively knew how to use these precious gems to enhance their health, and set in crowns, tiaras and goblets, jewels have been adopted by royalty to radiate their power. Practitioners of Chinese medicine are still using rose quartz on the tip of acupuncture needles to deepen the healing process.

Instinctively we know that there is something special about these colorful and wondrous natural gems – Crystal Meditation is probably one of the reasons you picked up this book, right? Crystals are forever, but this buzz may be new to you.

Perhaps you've been given a piece or you've got a chunk sitting on your desk as you were told it will stop that ever-growing 'negativity' virus. Maybe you wear the most precious of crystals within a ring to reflect the value of your love. Or maybe you've read about the beauty of crystals in a magazine, or they've danced in their thousands across your Instafeed. Maybe you like the color and the shape, the way they feel but you don't really know why. However you use them, however they call to you – it's all good.

GETTING INTO THE VIBE

We live in a world of constant shift, vibration and energy. The world is powered by a flaming ball of energy at its very core and a flaming ball of energy in the skies. This energy cannot be missed – even when it cannot be seen, it can be felt. And we are the same. We – our spirit, our life force – are all about energy: energy channellers, energy magnets, energy sponges, energy enhancers, energy seekers, energy, energy, energy and then some. The whole world is made of energy – every person, every object is vibrating at different frequencies. When we are happy and buzzing, we emit high vibes, and when we are burnt out and down we emit low vibes. Energy is fluid and changeable, and we can use crystals to change this energy and align ourselves with the vibe we desire.

RAISE YOUR VIBRATIONS

So, how do crystals work? We all know people who hype us up and chill us down, don't we? We all have a favorite shade of lipstick that gives us that extra zing, that trusted pair of pajamas that instantaneously makes us feel comfortable and 'at home'. Well, think of your crystals just like that – a bespoke tool kit – with each piece owning, harnessing, attracting and promoting its own special properties, its own power that resonates with your energy, your vibe, to aid you in a particular life event, moment or situation or to change, align or heighten your mood. Perhaps life is giving you a headache and you need some clarity; perhaps your heart feels broken but you're toying with jumping back on the dating horse and need some support and encouragement; or perhaps you're about to give the presentation of your life and are in much need of a power zap of confidence . . . Happy, sad, empowering, energizing – you name it, there is a crystal to support you.

Crystals are truly powerful: they work to heal or realign our energy – that vibe within and without us – when it's out of swing or to amplify and enhance good vibes – to help us feel more alive and to help bring within reach all those desires and goals we are hoping to fulfil. They are here to help us glow, to shine a light on those features of the self that we wish to heighten and brighten, but they're also here to teach us, to guide us, to work with us in the lifelong process of letting go of what no longer serves us.

CONNECTING CRYSTALS TO YOU AND YOUR LIFE

This book will help you to tap into your power by drawing on the energy of your crystals in your own personal practice. You can align yourself to their vibe by gently holding them while sitting in meditation, or adorning your energy centers, your chakras, while lying down. You can carry them with you in your everyday life: skin-on-skin is superbly powerful but crystals are strong enough to vibrate through your jeans or jacket pocket (if you're not yet ready to walk into a meeting and lay your crystal out with your day book in front of your boss). My pockets, my fingers, even my bra are full of them! My desk, my home, my kitchen sink are all glistening with them. Place them against parts of your body or on energy centers, and in areas of your life and home that need healing.

We can look at them and feel their warmth, much like a photo on the living-room wall that invokes a smile by reconnecting us with a good memory or a treasured time and place. We can take them into the bath and use the water to amplify their vibration; they can join us as a passenger in the car or on a plane when we're traveling far from home. We can put them on full display for the world to see or we can them keep them hidden away, tucked under our pillow just for us. Any way – as long as it works for you – is OK.

FINDING THE CRYSTAL THAT'S RIGHT FOR YOU

This book introduces you to over seventy different crystals and their various healing qualities. Each chapter is dedicated to a different aspect of day-to-day life. Together we shall search for the crystal that's right for you and your current concerns, whether you are aiming to achieve a personal or professional goal, seeking to change your mood, looking to enhance a great workout or just want a good night's sleep!

Pay attention to the alternative suggestions at the bottom of each entry. Everyone's energy and everyone's relationship with crystals is different, so it is definitely worth investing time in experimenting and exploring, learning which crystals speak to you, when and why. Feel free to jump to the indexes in the back for quick reference – there are no rules, no regulations – just dive in and go for it! **Just remeber crystals are complementary, not a replacement for any medical treatment you may be receiving. If in doubt, speak to your medical adviser.**

You will also find a guide to selecting and sourcing your crystals and advice on how to care for them. You'll develop ways of relating to and working with your crystals, through meditation, journaling and focusing on your chakras. Learn how to live with crystals and bring them into your everyday life – at home, at work, or by wearing them.

ARE YOU READY TO LIVE A HIGH-VIBE LIFE?

You may be somewhat doubtful, nervous or plain scared of exploring all that crystals have to offer – just in case you 'get it wrong', or fear of looking silly. I am no scientist, but I am a feeler, a hands-on healer, and I work intuitively with people as much as I do with crystals. My biggest discovery in my fifteen years of practice is to let this be a time of play and explore what works best for you, because that is really what it is all about. I am so excited to be joining you as you enter the wonderful world of crystals!

The true magic of crystals is their affinity with the individual. Much like your mood, your needs and your desires, your crystal of choice will change, perhaps daily, determined by mood, by event, by the inevitable changes in your life. So it's a good idea to have a staple kit of go-to crystals for most eventualities. Try thinking of it like your closest friendship circle: you may have thousands of friends on social media, but when it really comes down to it, there are only five or six you would count on as your 'go-tos'. Each person in that group has a trait that you lean on in times of heartache, or when looking for fun, or when you need a confidence boost, sound advice or a good hug. This is how crystals call to me, like a friend in time of pleasure, pain, need or joy. Without even thinking about it I know exactly who to turn to and where to go.

HOW TO
SELECT
YOUR
CRYSTALS

Discovering your rocks

So, how do you know which crystals to pick? How do you pick your crystal of the day? Is it one a day? Or one a week? Can you carry more than one at any one time? And – most importantly – how do you know what is 'right' for you? There are no real rules here, only guides. You need to trust your instinct and that comes with practice; tune in more deeply to your feelings and pay attention to the energy, the vibes, the communication you are receiving from the crystals.

I liken the selection process to getting dressed in the morning. Often you know exactly the look you want for the day ahead and you have your go-to outfits, the comfy wear, the outdoor wear. Sometimes this is spot on: this is your 'knowing', your intuition, guiding you. Sometimes, however, you pop on what you have planned and it just doesn't feel right. It's the same with your crystals – you know exactly what needs shifting or enhancing and you turn the pages here to find what you need, and then you go to what you thought you needed and the vibe just isn't there. You are 'just not feeling it today'. How many times have we said that? It's not to say it doesn't work, just that you may need to take a different tack.

HOW MANY CRYSTALS DO YOU NEED?

You can have as many or as few as you like. You can have many of the same crystal – it's only natural to have a favorite. Allow your squad to expand organically: having twenty crystals rather than one will not make things move any more quickly. What you put in you will get out no matter the size or the scale.

HOW MANY TYPES OF CRYSTAL ARE THERE?

There are seven types of crystal or crystal systems but over two thousand forms and counting. Some formations have multiple colors and each color has its own specific healing property – there is something for everyone.

DOES IT MATTER HOW BIG OR SMALL YOUR CRYSTALS ARE?

Size is not a factor. Just as with human beings, a piece can be small and mighty and can have a greater vibration than that of a giant raw rock. I might hold a piece and feel the world from it; you might hold it and feel nothing. The connection is what matters – that click you get when you meet.

WHERE DO YOU START?

We must always start with intention. If you are going into a working week with a packed schedule, big goals to achieve and a tight deadline, or if you've a date pending and you're excited but nervous of the unknown – whatever it is, all you need to do is ask yourself: what is it you really want? Use this book instinctively, flick through the pages to see what catches your eye, or search the index, and look for what's inspiring you, troubling you, what it is you want to heal or what it is you want to empower.

Everyone's energy is different, and everyone's relation-ship with crystals is different, so play around and see what works for you. Use this book as a guide, but always listen to your own instincts too. I am a *huge* devotee of tiger's eye – it delivers me bountiful confidence when on the precipice of fear. My sister, however, when prescribed tiger's eye and

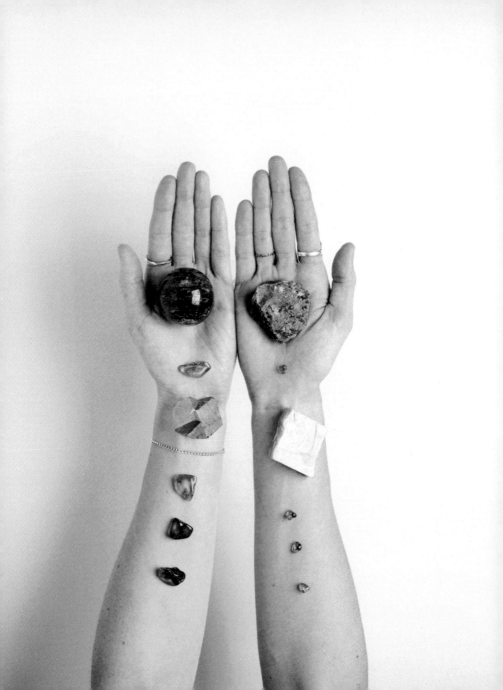

jet for the same goal, will lean without question towards jet, because that's what's right for her. That's why I have included alternative crystal suggestions at the end of each entry.

WRITE IT DOWN

Start cataloguing, journaling, or photographically logging. The best way to work out what's working for you is to keep a record and consult past experience. What helped you when? Crystal journaling is your own self-help or how-to guide. Documenting how one crystal made you feel as opposed to another when you were in a particular state or mood can be really powerful. If after a time a crystal isn't giving you what you need, don't get frustrated, just set it aside, cleanse it and try something new. Crystals will not judge you – your loyalty to one will never be called into question – but how will you grow if you don't experiment with nature's abundant variety?

How you feel on the day will ultimately sway you into your selection process. Here are a few ways to try.

GETTING A FEEL FOR IT

You might be feeling particularly playful or, on the other hand, in a state of profound procrastination. Feel your way to what you need. You are likely to discover what you are looking for through your own compass, your own intuition.

Place your crystal team into a line-up. I would suggest creating a crystal arc, like a rainbow, in front of you. Rub your hands together gently three times to stimulate the chakra points at the center of your hands, and then move your dominant hand over the arc, right to left. Take long deep breaths and gently close your eyes. This sense of turning within will give you greater response to the stimulation from without. Now turn to your intention. Asking is important. The words don't have to be exact; you'll find your voice by simply giving life to it:

Please guide me to what I need.
I am confident of the selection made for me.
Crystal, hear my call. I am feeling tired/stressed/etc.
I want to . . .

Lightly float your hand left to right and right to left. Keep it moving back and forth. Think of a treasure hunter scanning the beach with a metal detector – your hand provides the feedback. Concentrate on deep, slow breathing, repeating your intention, giving yourself time. Move your mind towards declarations of 'I feel you', or, 'I connect with you by my hand and from my heart.' Sometimes I feel a gentle prickling when my hand passes over what I need. Sometimes it's a gentle breeze – sometimes hot, sometimes cool – passing between us. If doubt sneaks in, ask for confirmation, scan again, resist the temptation to take a peek and then lower your hand to where you've been drawn. If your hand lands on two crystals, that's fine. Either take both or return to the scanning process, this time passing your hand between the two.

GO FOR THE GRAB

This for me is truly visual and instinct-based. You know when you see something in a store and buy it because 'it's just talking to me, I have to have it'? Whatever the 'it' is, if it's just glinting at you in the right way at that moment, it's meant to be. Close your eyes for a split second and whisper, 'Show me what I need.' The piece will glint at you or your eye will be drawn to a particular stone. You'll know when your heart says, 'This is it', 'I need you', or you simply want to smile.

As to how many crystals you can have on any one given day, that's up to you. Self-empowerment, remember, comes in part from listening to yourself, from trusting your gut. Crystals – just like your friends – don't cancel each other out; they work with each other, as a team.

I believe it is important to have a go-to buddy network, a tribe, a gang – whatever you want to call it. I have a go-to set of crystals – stones that have become reliable healers. How do I know who the go-to gang are for me? I spend time with them and I nurture our connection and relationship. So pick and choose and apply the information that follows as *you* feel best fits; swap a crystal in and out, but *only* after first giving it a little bit of time to call back to you.

Say you are packing to go on vacation or bolting out the door because life has decided to run at a hectic pace without prior warning – these will be the essential crystals you need. Everyone's tribe will be different, but here are the classics to which most people feel an affinity.

YOUR GO-TO CRYSTAL SUPER SET

Rose Quartz

TO EMBRACE AND LOVE YOUR TRUE SELF

The stone of the heart . . . your heart, my heart, the heart of life. Much like its floral namesake, this beautiful, warming crystal stimulates and pulses out pure, radiating, unconditional, compassionate love. Polished or raw, held or carried as a palm stone or a pocket stone, or placed under your pillow or by your bed, this soft, peaceful pink stone seeks to heighten and optimize love within you, encouraging love into the very essence of 'self' and allowing you to comfortably explore love within the everyday. Rose quartz acts as a compass of the heart, guiding you lovingly to where it feels you need to be in order to grow and expand to your purest potential. If your ego or your mind is stressing you out or screaming at you to move in a potential misdirection, you need never fear while your loving friend is here. When you wish to feel the love of life within your heart and bones, when you long for romantic love to come a-knocking, and when you yearn for compassion in dealing with what can seem to be overwhelming events, allow her to work with you.

Tiger's Eye
FOR INNER STRENGTH AND CONFIDENCE

The protector and ultimate confidence booster – moving you and allowing you to see through your doubt, through your darkest shadows, to the burning point of pure raw passion. Tiger's eye fires up that passion in the everyday, bridging the challenges of fear and old doubts. The red-brown and golden tiger's eye is the trusted bodyguard, enabling you to move through your day in a calm, inspired fashion, cloaked in confidence. Tiger's eye promotes the sharpness of our inner sight, so that we can see things as they really are. It strengthens us in times of change. This is the stone to take with you to an impending big meeting, to that terrifying first date, or on those days when you're in need of some grounding in the present, in situations when you're afraid of falling over your own two feet. Allow tiger's eye to help you to witness your own strength and to carry it proudly into the day.

Amethyst
TO SOOTHE YOUR SOUL WITH CLARITY AND CALM

This visually stunning, rich purple crystal enhances our control of our emotional river, promoting a balance within our inner emotions. It reminds us that our sensitivities – when harnessed – can become our greatest allies; balancing these, it prevents us becoming 'drunk' with feeling or 'drowning' during an 'emotional flood'. What's more, this stone allows us to lift the delicate veil between the physical world and the spiritual world, channelling our emotions into a bridge to the 'beyond' to allow us to seek heightened spiritual and emotional experiences. Not sure how to handle a tricky situation? Need clarity on making a big decision but don't know who to turn to for advice? Then turn to amethyst and she will lull you into a peaceful state, so that life can answer your call. This is perhaps my absolute favorite.

Citrine
TO DANCE IN JOY AND SWIM IN SUCCESS

This sunshine-yellow crystal is the skeleton key to abundance. This doesn't just mean bringing in the big bucks . . . it's all success: financial, professional or personal. Much like the sun burning through gray clouds, citrine burns off negativity: it's a great piece for the home to disperse the lingering hangover of an argument, to enrich your purse and your pockets, and to nourish you at the core of your very being, tapping into the abundance of your own joyful, fortunate vibrations.

Clear Quartz
FOR MEGA HIGH-VIBING

This may be an incredibly common crystal on our planet, but it's not one that should be overlooked nor discounted. We often get 'lost' – sometimes life throws us in a spin without warning, we feel we've lost our sense of self and purpose, and the night-time blues leak deeper into the days. When experiencing this discombobulation, we feel the need to turn to our inner compass to seek something 'special' to lift our spirits. However, what we really need is rippling through the ground at our feet. Let us remember there is great strength in numbers. This enlightening stone, with its supersonic high vibration, allows us to rise above the noise and daily chatter to a heightened state of connectivity with self and spirit. If ever there was a need for you to feel life vibing you back, this is without question the stone to provide it.

Inner peace and inner calm are states of being – often we reach to outside ourselves and grab on to people or things to enhance a state of calm amidst our lives' storms – when what we really need is tether back to our own harbor to find that often-mentioned 'peace of mind'. What may be traumatic for you today may be a walk in the park tomorrow and what rocks your boat may be different for another, so here are some crystals that can help empower you and champion you through various states you may be seeking to overcome.

CRYSTALS FOR INNER PEACE AND CALM

Blue Lace Agate
FOR DISSOLVING STRESSFUL STATES OF MIND

Much like the cloud it resembles, this precious, light blue and white-laced crystal allows you to soften and gracefully dissolve negative frames of mind and heart. Blue lace agate will work to stimulate and elevate your mind, restoring peace, enhancing and realigning your communication with yourself and others, and restoring you to a place of truth and empowered positivity. This is a crystal for when we are tired or stress is creeping in and suffocating us, when we grasp at words and actions blindly to make our way through, throwing them out when we do not mean to, hurting not just others but ourselves. If you are feeling lost for words and looking for a release from the weight of negativity, this is the crystal for you.

OTHER CRYSTALS WITH SIMILAR PROPERTIES: lapis lazuli, clear quartz, opal

Jet
FOR PROTECTION AND ABSORBING NEGATIVE ENERGY

The jet-black crystal is the stone of the night – redefining this as a time not of intimidating darkness but of powerful, energizing purification. Jet projects a protective vibration, absorbing negativity from the root of matter, gently soaking up 'bad vibes' and soothing the sense of unease that sets in when you hold on to tension. Jet works much like a sponge, so that stress no longer spills into your waking day, allowing you to walk tall. Perhaps you've a newfound spring in your step but it's caused some tension with your best pal, partner or colleague, when they should be embracing this change. On the surface, they are trying to be happy for you, but you sense that deep down they're struggling. Rather than being affected by this, you can use jet to envelop you, to soak up and dissolve toxic energy, so that you can continue to grow.

OTHER CRYSTALS WITH SIMILAR PROPERTIES: lepidolite, smoky quartz, tiger's eye

Jade
FOR SERENITY AND AN OPEN HEART

Jade comes in multiple, beautiful colors, all with their own special properties. The nurturing green jade is a deeply purifying, stabilizing stone that seeks to channel serenity while enhancing your intuition – your sense of knowing without knowing *how* you know, which is born from our hearts rather than learned. Use this crystal when you are feeling overwhelmed by any emotion – positive or negative – as its maternal nurturing qualities warm and assist in the safe

destruction of painful or unhelpful emotions. Rub it on your third eye, forehead or temples to release tension headaches.

OTHER CRYSTALS WITH SIMILAR PROPERTIES: celestite, moonstone, peridot, rose quartz

Clear Quartz
FOR A CLEARER VIEW

The high-vibing clear quartz allows us to keep our feet on the ground and raise our minds in order to cut through the veils of self-doubt – dramatic, painful, habitual, repetitive thoughts and stresses that make us feel blue or low. Clear quartz enables us to reconnect with a greater sense of self by encouraging us to view real life through its crystal-clear and laser-sharp lens. In current times, we look to be seen and accepted more and more by connecting through pictures of ourselves – we get a short-lived kick from social 'likes' and digital love hearts, finding ourselves tied to a spinning wheel of social approval and neglect. Turn to quartz for a long-lasting 'like' from within; see yourself and allow yourself to be truly seen. Clear quartz is a trusted friend when you are seeking to feel greater connectivity with self and spirit.

OTHER CRYSTALS WITH SIMILAR PROPERTIES: amethyst, celestite, citrine, opal

Citrine

FOR CULTIVATING YOUR OWN SUNSHINE

Think of citrine as a sunflower in a field. Much like the flower, citrine stretches and opens our hearts, turning heart, head and self towards the warm rays of life. Work with this stone to overcome self-made obstacles of the mind, to remind yourself how to swim in joy when you feel you are being dragged down beneath the surface of life's river. Perhaps you're dancing into work after a fun-filled weekend that's left you on a high, but the environment in the office doesn't reflect your present state of being. Rather than vibing down to that level, open your heart and blaze that sunshine to raise the room higher – everyone wins when we share our light!

OTHER CRYSTALS WITH SIMILAR PROPERTIES: quartz, rhodonite, rose quartz, sunstone

Aventurine

FOR CALMING ANGER AND IRRITATION

This deeply enriching green stone should be used to help you to root deep in tranquility, promoting blissful mental stability. Calming anger and irritation within and without, this precious vibration works to align and balance your central nervous system, much like hitting the reset

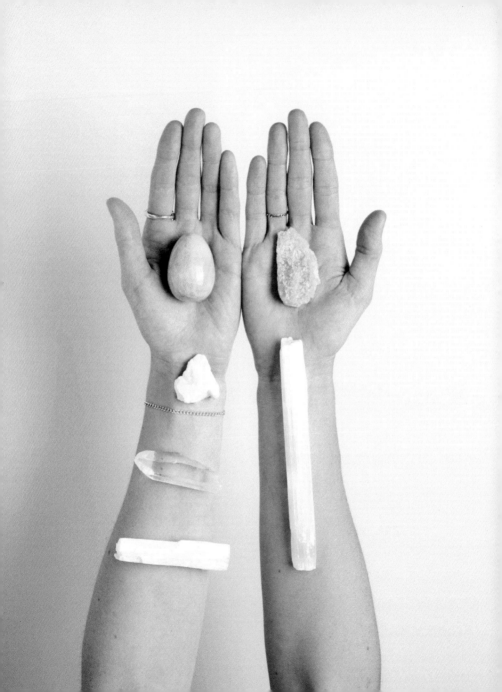

button. This stone takes the weight of the world from you and returns you to a peaceful state of mind. Someone pushed you on the subway, raced ahead of you to grab the last seat on the bus, walked into you while mindlessly immersed in their phone? Or someone stole your idea at the office and claimed it as their own? Rather than calling out 'This is unfair!', take aventurine in your hand and rub it with your thumb, each rub becoming more and more gentle as the storm tempers and dissolves, before you broadcast it out loud.

OTHER CRYSTALS WITH SIMILAR PROPERTIES: abalone, amazonite, amethyst, sugilite

Celestite
FOR SPIRITUAL GUIDANCE AND ENHANCING DIVINE POWER

Whenever you want to feel the serenity of divine power or call to the skies for spiritual guidance; whenever life leaves you no choice but to turn to something much, much bigger than yourself; whenever you need to feel that power, that presence, and to take flight within, then this beautiful creamy-white crystal is the stone for you. It is a magical stress reliever. When life is racing by at a hundred miles an hour and it feels as though things are moving increasingly out of your control, ask celestite to embrace you in a warm, energetic hug. This is a go-to crystal for times in which you need to surrender to the unknown, that divine power, that great architect in the sky. A stone for the home to generate warmth, protection and possibility.

OTHER CRYSTALS WITH SIMILAR PROPERTIES: amethyst, jade, lapis lazuli, malachite

Blue Calcite
FOR ABSORBING FRUSTRATION

Blue calcite is a remarkable crystal. As our liver purifies our blood for recirculation, blue calcite absorbs and filters energy to make it beneficial to us. If you're feeling lost at sea, allow blue calcite to make a life raft out of the drama. Lean into this pillow of a stone to rest your weary head, and make way for its soft, relaxing and recuperative touch. Blue calcite is used to support your blood pressure, so if the day has left you frustrated and enraged, soothe yourself with its magic.

OTHER CRYSTALS WITH SIMILAR PROPERTIES: angelite, jade, onyx, turquoise

Have you ever considered just how much of your day – your life – is spent at work? You don't need me to tell you that you have to make these days really count and you need to draw from them what *you* need, what makes you come to life, what makes you feel empowered. But perhaps you need some help working out what makes you flourish, or how to make yourself glow that little bit brighter in a somewhat crowded room, how to own your success and allow it to drive you happily and confidently forward. Here are some new colleagues, a support system to help you grab life and shine in your place of work, whatever your role may be.

CRYSTALS FOR KICKING BUTT AT WORK

Fluorite

FOR REDUCING NOISE AND GETTING ORGANIZED

Fluorite is a wonderful noise-reducer and organizational influencer. It is born in many colors: green, blue, purple, yellow and brown. Seek this crystal when looking to dial down loud outside mental influences and chitter-chatter and to fix on heightened mental clarity. Fluorite promotes the sharpening of the strongest tools in your set – enhancing your learning, self-confidence, organization and general ability to structure everyday life. It's one to keep in your office top drawer.

OTHER CRYSTALS WITH SIMILAR PROPERTIES: aventurine, clear quartz, hematite, tiger's eye

Hematite

FOR FOCUS AND CONCENTRATION

Used by the ancient Egyptians for mirrors, hematite is a mystical silver crystal. Its reflective and magnetic properties focus you when you are faced with challenges, helping you to concentrate and bring conviction and attention to

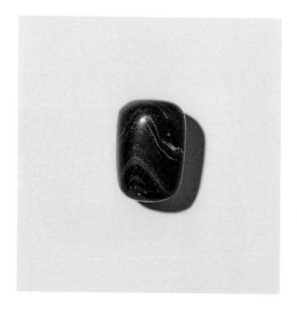

what's high on the to-do list when perhaps you're feeling over-powered or timid in times of challenge or unexpected criticism. Hematite allows you to learn from these situations and get stuck back in to work or study, to focus on the big picture and your main goals without feeling smothered by the little details.

OTHER CRYSTALS WITH SIMILAR PROPERTIES: blue kyanite, obsidian, jet

Tiger's Eye
FOR GLOWING IN CREATIVITY

Tiger's eye is the keeper of confidence. Displaying itself in a beautiful brown and yellow – also sometimes in pink, blue and red – this stealthy stone frees blocked creativity and helps you get yourself and your mind down to work. Use it when you are feeling stretched thin or scatty, to feel super-committed to the tasks at hand, and then watch those plates spin with precision. Use tiger's eye to give yourself confidence and passion in creative brainstorms or in conversations about your future. Allow it to help you untie your tongue and get creative in your communication.

OTHER CRYSTALS WITH SIMILAR PROPERTIES: agate, amethyst, aventurine, labradorite, ruby

Turquoise
FOR EMPOWERING COMMUNICATION

The vivid blue, teal or green stone turquoise is the master of communication. Turquoise encourages you to locate and take hold of the reins of self. Not sure how to 'be you' in the office? Then turquoise will work with you to allow your talents to show without fear of embarrassment or rejection. Allow turquoise to assist you not only in speaking your truth but in hearing others. It will help you flourish as you lead and establish a strong position within a team. Equally, turquoise vibes down the interference of technology and balances your mood, promotes clarity to allow for sharp decision-making, boosts energy when you are feeling exhausted or prey to stress and worry – all at the same time. A true game-changer!

OTHER CRYSTALS WITH SIMILAR PROPERTIES: blue kyanite, blue lace agate, iolite, tiger's eye

Ruby
FOR POWERING UP, COMMITTING TO THE TASK
AND GETTING THE JOB DONE

The enriching ruby and its powerful warming red tone – much like the flickering of a candle or fire – promotes a long-lasting, long-burning, well-fueled and hugely

energizing vibe, while calming you into a natural state of confidence. Use this gemstone to feel the courage of a lion in your heart, to hold onto your self-esteem as you gently and confidently explore and share your passion. A crystal for protection, guarding you from gossip so that you can bravely go your own way.

OTHER CRYSTALS WITH SIMILAR PROPERTIES: garnet, hematite, tiger's eye

Chrysocolla
FOR REKINDLING YOUR PASSION AND SELF-MOTIVATION

Keeping cool and carrying on is a must during your working day and chrysocolla can act as your trusty sidekick, deflecting and discharging negativity – from man and machine! This is a real all-around team player as far as crystals go – not only calming, but energising, reducing self-doubt while engaging confidence, enhancing your personal power while focusing your lens to become aware of and support your needs. Equally, chrysocolla is a stone of rebirth, so if you are in need of giving life to a seemingly stagnant role, call on this to help you breathe fresh air into tiresome tasks.

OTHER CRYSTALS WITH SIMILAR PROPERTIES: rose quartz, hematite, tiger's eye, jet, snowflake obsidian

Rainforest Jasper
FOR ACHIEVING SUCCESS AND OPENING DOORS

Peace, happiness, success and a healthy cash flow – how many of these are on your 'yes, please' list? You're in luck: rainforest jasper is a game-changer – a keen promoter and enabler of them all. Call on this treasure-chest opener to feel invigorated and charged up, ready to get stuck into and aligned with a task at hand when tiredness or a post-heavy-lunch slump creep in. Want that promotion, want to make the next big move, want to relocate, want to take a risk? Use rainforest jasper to open doors and have confidence that what's behind them will be more than worth your while.

OTHER CRYSTALS WITH SIMILAR PROPERTIES: amber, golden healer quartz, angelite, sapphire, turquoise

We reflect on the outside who we are on the inside, and vice versa. Healthy energy is as important as a healthy diet, a healthy mindset, glowing skin and strong body. When we feel out of balance, when we've had a 'big night', when we've sat too long at the computer screen, or when we're fighting against the light that draws us to explore the contents of our fridge – all sorts of crazy can start to happen. Life can sometimes be hard to digest and we suppress our emotions internally, creating a sense of unease that has a chaotic effect on our outer world. Here are some support systems to give you extra willpower when you've over-indulged (and why not!), for when your body needs a little extra TLC or you need a bit of a treat and comfort, but are trying to stay away from the booze or the kitchen cupboards.

CRYSTALS
FOR
FEELING
GREAT ON
THE INSIDE

Smoky Quartz
FOR THE DETOX

Born from our quartz collective, smoky quartz – like its siblings – is a high-vibing hard-working crystal that excels when used in internal cleansing. Smoky quartz is the cheerleader of the kidneys – helping us flush out unwanted toxins – so it is a perfect partner for a good sweat-out session in the gym or relaxation in the sauna. I would recommend it as a grounding stone when you are participating in high-intensity training to keep you centered on the challenge at hand, clearing away the negativity of the mind when it chatters to you that 'you can't', so you can have fun while showing yourself that you *can*.

OTHER CRYSTALS WITH SIMILAR PROPERTIES: blue apatite, opal, beryl

Blue Apatite
FOR KICKING CONSTANT CRAVINGS

Apatite is a stone of results – and will work with you so you have the patience to feel and see them. If you are seeking some goal-orientated assistance in your regime, blue apatite is your go-to crystal. When you are feeling picky and searching for some comfort in the kitchen cupboards, it aids not only in suppressing those cravings but also in promoting a speedy metabolic rate and a breakdown of proteins. Blue apatite will also motivate you on those mornings when the duvet seems more appealing than the fresh air on your face from the morning run or the loud beats of the gym class you've paid for but emotionally only half-heartedly committed to.

OTHER CRYSTALS WITH SIMILAR PROPERTIES: aventurine, jet, clear quartz, rose quartz

Bloodstone
FOR REVITALISING YOUR IMMUNE SYSTEM

The bewilderingly beautiful red-green crystal bloodstone is one to seek out when the flu or a cold kicks in, or you're generally under the weather. Bloodstone is the perfect partner for your immune system when life demands necessary periods of rest and repair. It gently alleviates negativity and raises your energy levels to give you extra strength to blast through fatigue. A go-to staple stone for re-aligning 'you', getting you match fit and back on track.

OTHER CRYSTALS WITH SIMILAR PROPERTIES: aventurine, carnelian, coral

Garnet

FOR RECOVERY AND RE-ENERGISING (AND CURING HANGOVERS)

Garnet is an almighty crystal that can call to you in many colors: red, pink, green, orange, yellow, brown and black. It works wonders on the recovery process, stimulating your regeneration in a physical and metaphysical level. Garnet supports you in the resting process, purifying your energy and drawing in new energy when your resources are depleted. Garnet is a stone of the heart and will get your blood pumping. If you've a big sporting challenge ahead of you, garnet will promote the luck needed to support you and your hard work in achieving your goals. It will also soothe the self-inflicted hangover!

OTHER CRYSTALS WITH SIMILAR PROPERTIES: amethyst, jet, lepidolite, tiger's eye

Lepidolite

FOR TENSION RELEASE

It's important that we feel not only mental strength but internal and physical strength. Lepidolite, in its lilac/rose/violet hues, will work to support you. If you have a need to bend and flex in a new direction or you are being haunted by an old ailment, the magic of lepidolite will work with your joints and ease long-held tension. Similarly, lepidolite will support you as you overcome addictions of all kinds.

OTHER CRYSTALS WITH SIMILAR PROPERTIES: blue lace agate, onyx, smoky quartz

Onyx
FOR PMA

PMA, a positive mental attitude is sometimes a challenging state of mind to achieve. Call onyx into play so that it can transmute the negative into the positive, spring-cleaning your mind of internal chatter to allow for a clearer view of the world, making the best of an unhealthy situation. Onyx is a sensational detoxifying crystal and seeks to dispel negative energy rather than soak it up.

OTHER CRYSTALS WITH SIMILAR PROPERTIES: lepidolite, malachite*, opal, tiger's eye

*Please use malachite for only short periods of time. Twenty minutes with malachite should be followed by at least ten minutes with a soothing stone such as rose quartz.

What makes you beautiful? In fact, what is beauty? It's not what you see but how you feel. It starts from the inside and it shines out. Feeling beautiful allows you to let go of negative thoughts about your blemishes or scars, whatever your hang-ups, to see past them to *you*. Whatever you look like, whatever society tells you, you are beautiful. So how do we magnify all these things that make us beautiful?

CRYSTALS FOR RADIATING ON THE OUTSIDE

Rhodochrosite

TO RADIATE AND GLOW AND BRING LIFE TO YOUR SKIN

The warming and comforting pink and orange tones of rhodochrosite will help you master one of the most important things in life: the pure selfless love that without question looks beautiful on everyone. So why not wear it and wear it well? Rhodochrosite is the glowing queen of rejuvenation – for your skin, your hair, your follicles, your nail beds. She will assist in regenerating, soothing and enhancing, giving you a high glow and high gloss. A great piece to add to your beauty kit, to keep under your pillow, by your bedside or in your bathroom – all those places where you allow yourself time to deepen your glow.

OTHER CRYSTALS WITH SIMILAR PROPERTIES: carnelian, labradorite, rose quartz

Labradorite

FOR RAISING THE ROOF ON YOUR SELF-ESTEEM

Labradorite is the perfect reflector – showing you as you look in life, not as you do according to your ego. Labradorite energises you as it delves in to your heart and soul, bringing out all the goodness from within, with every heartbeat raising your self-esteem and allowing you to embrace your attractive glow. Labradorite is the master of removal and dispelling – removing unwanted energies from your aura or your inner being, heightening your energetic make-up and innate qualities to their most attractive and dispelling myths about your looks and those features you hold in a low regard. Hold hands with labradorite to help you hold hands with yourself: it will show you your beauty in its truest form and encourage you to regard yourself warmly, lovingly and honestly when looking at your reflection in the mirror. Powerful to say the least!

OTHER CRYSTALS WITH SIMILAR PROPERTIES: apatite, citrine, moss agate, tiger's eye

Rose Quartz
FOR SOOTHING ACNE AND PROMOTING CLEAR SKIN

There is a reason most people have heard of, owned or been given a piece of nature's soft, dewy, candy-floss pink rose quartz. It's not because it's common; it's because it's the very best in her field: love. A heart-filled stone that can be used to soothe acne by targeting the emotional root of its inflammation, as you slumber she will open your heart and send you into a protective and deeply energizing 'beauty sleep'. Work with her to radiate love from every pore, and to attract love back. For a more hands-on approach, you can gently rub your skin with the smooth edge of rose quartz (stay clear of touching angry skin) and she will

radiate to the troubled or problem areas. Or try using a rose-quartz candle-holder to allow the rose quartz to reflect the candlelight to give you a freshly-kissed-all-over look and feel.

OTHER CRYSTALS WITH SIMILAR PROPERTIES: azurite, ruby, selenite

Carnelian
FOR A YOUTHFUL GLOW

Vitality and life force are key factors in anti-ageing. The warmth of the luxurious carnelian crystal – red, orange, pink or brown – works to harmonize you with the natural ageing process, rather than encouraging you to try and fight it. Carnelian touches you by soothing and caressing the delicate and precious tissues across your entire body. It also heightens the absorption of vitamins and minerals, taken orally or applied to the skin – a wonder to work into your daily skin-care routine!

OTHER CRYSTALS WITH SIMILAR PROPERTIES: aventurine, jade, peridot, rose quartz

Crazy Lace Agate
FOR LAUGHTER (HAPPY IS HEALTHY!)

The energy of laughter is a beautiful thing and adorns us with an attractive glow as it pours through us. Crazy lace agate is adorned with the most fabulous title of 'life's laughter stone'. It is a champion of joy and confidence, promotes optimism and helps you strive towards stability in life and self. Allow her to wrap you in a magnetic field of beautifying happiness and people will swarm to you for all the right reasons. If you are feeling fierce, attractive and powerful, allow crazy lace to be like your setting spray to hold the look. Please use in short stints so as not to get too drunk on life and out of balance!

OTHER CRYSTALS WITH SIMILAR PROPERTIES: apatite, aventurine, citrine, diamond

Apache Tear
FOR BODY AND BEAUTY INTELLIGENCE

If you are looking for a dance partner in life, Apache tear is your girl – acting as an energy diffuser for even the shyest of us. Apache tear entices those innate qualities that so rarely surface: she encourages the true you, with all your strength and compassion. Take your place on the dance floor and invite other nervous souls to join you there! If you're looking for spontaneity, to be free of self-limitation, she is your friend.

OTHER CRYSTALS WITH SIMILAR PROPERTIES: labradorite, moonstone, rhodochrosite, rose quartz

Azurite
FOR EXPLORING AND DISCOVERING TRUE BEAUTY

In order to look good on the outside we need to explore how we recognise beauty within ourselves. Here we can call to the deep-blue depths of azurite. Azurite gently guides us towards a true awareness of self, breaking down and working through self-criticism in order to harness a positive and empowered perspective. Do you believe your ears are too big or your boobs and butt are too small? Your mom and your friends say the opposite, but they're only saying that because they have to, right? Wrong! It's because you've built a wall of distorted perceptions about yourself. Azurite will allow accurate self-perception to emerge: honest, true and owned by you.

OTHER CRYSTALS WITH SIMILAR PROPERTIES: labradorite, lepidolite, moss agate, rose quartz, tiger's eye

Falling in love with yourself is no mean feat: just as we overcome one barrier in the never-ending series of self-awareness hurdles, another often flies towards us. To cultivate love within we have to take hold of what makes us happy, to take hold of our minds, to open up bravely and expand into ourselves and allow that process to flood into our everyday lives. Owning, respecting and treasuring ourselves, like cherished pearls, is not selfish; it is strengthening. It allows us to embrace others as we embrace ourselves – and that is true love.

CRYSTALS FOR SELF LOVE AND CARE

Rose Quartz
TO LOVE UNCONDITIONALLY

We cannot *not* start our exploration without holding hands with the queen of hearts – rose quartz, our teacher of unconditional love. Love is an energy, a vibration, and one we often seek too far outside ourselves. Rose quartz reminds us that the greatest love of all starts from within. She will act as your ever-faithful, ever-loyal guide, steering you through your exploration of this purest of energies, from the very heart of yourself, softening negative habits and patterns that reduce you and hold you back from your full potential. Take rose quartz to heart and work with her in setting positive affirmations and intentions. Use her when you are feeling that you cannot be held, so as to remove and dispel the fear that you are unlovable.

OTHER CRYSTALS WITH SIMILAR PROPERTIES: golden healer quartz, labradorite, sunstone

Peridot
FOR BRINGING IT BEAUTIFULLY BACK TO YOU

Inner love is not, as society so often leads us to believe, a form of arrogance. It is self-worth, self-value, self-respect – holding up the self in its best light – in all its glory and greatness. Often the value we place on these qualities dips or rises in relation to past choices or current surroundings. Peridot may be small, but it is mighty when it comes to healing matters of the heart. Work with it to enhance the cleansing of the negativity shrouding your heart – from past mistakes or from intentionally cruel words. Let it expand your heart like a beautiful lotus flower reborn from muddy waters, facing the sun in joy through gentle forgiveness.

OTHER CRYSTALS WITH SIMILAR PROPERTIES: hematite, moonstone, tiger's eye

Turquoise
FOR SETTING THOSE DEMONS FREE

Turquoise – dreamy blue or green – should be held when you sense the saboteurs creeping up on your heels. These saboteurs can be fears built in your mind or people embodying those fears. We've all experienced a back-handed compliment or heard words dipped in venom, haven't we? We've probably consciously and subconsciously delivered a few ourselves – perhaps even *to* ourselves. Work with the kindness promoted by

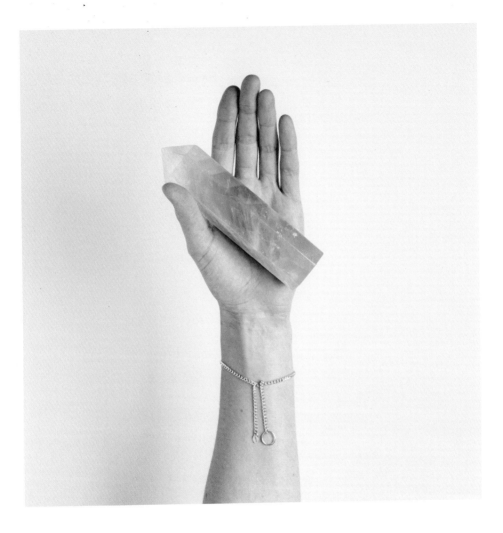

turquoise to cut off sabotage at the root, not just to ward off its shadow for short-term effect. It will temper your mood swings and encourage calm exploration as you reach out to commit to or ask for love.

OTHER CRYSTALS WITH SIMILAR PROPERTIES: aragonite, iolite, onyx, rose quartz

Kunzite
FOR ALIGNING, INSPIRING AND EXTERNALIZING YOUR INNER POWER

In order to feel love or develop love from within we need to align to what that word 'love' means to us. Kunzite is a friend who will pick you up, encourage you to walk through the hurt and return you to your life track. Often in life we can feel rejected and it takes time to get us back on our feet, to feel brave enough to open up to a lover or to reconnect with a friend who you might feel has done you wrong. Kunzite will assist by aligning your heart with your throat, so that you can speak your truth with a loving, knowing and captivating authority, so that you can make peace or you can let go. When looking for new lovers or friends, kunzite should be used to open the door to your heart and inspire you to make deep, emotionally rewarding connections at every level.

OTHER CRYSTALS WITH SIMILAR PROPERTIES: blue turquoise, lapis lazuli, rose quartz

Tourmaline

FOR SOAKING YOUR SOUL

Sometimes we feel a tiredness that goes deeper than our bones: we feel uncharacteristically cloudy, hazy and lazy; the tiredness is in our soul. Embracing tourmaline is much like taking a bath after a long day. Use the heart-transformer tourmaline – black, brown, green, pink, yellow or blue – to unwind and soak off the dirt, to purify yourself as water cleanses your skin. Gently clarifying layer by layer, tourmaline will turn the seemingly grey back into bright vivid colour. Use it not just when you feel blue, but as part of your weekly regime to keep yourself beaming from within.

OTHER CRYSTALS WITH SIMILAR PROPERTIES: amethyst, aragonite, sapphire

Rhodonite

FOR INTERNAL BALANCE

When we love, we operate in a state of imperfect give and take. The pink or red rhodonite allows us to perform circus tricks of the heart, balancing us between the highs and the lows, healing emotional shock when we take a fall from the high wire and supporting us as we climb back to the top. Use rhodonite to help you forgive yourself when

you feel like beating yourself up for making 'poor choices' or 'mistakes'. It will remind you that in order to truly enjoy the highs, you must sometimes explore the lows, and she will help you take both in your stride.

OTHER CRYSTALS WITH SIMILAR PROPERTIES: pietersite, rose quartz, selenite, tiger's eye

Prasiolite
TO LOVE THE SHADE AND THE SHADOW

In order to fully love ourselves we need to accept every shade of self. We often say, 'If I could change this about myself . . .', or, 'I'd be better if my nose were smaller, my legs longer, my hair blonder . . .' Or we have conversations in our heads, saying, 'I'm a fake, I'm a phony', or, 'What happens when they see the real me, when I get found out?' Prasiolite will cradle you and empower you as you work together to remove negativity blocks based in low-level thinking and self-doubt. Loving is raw and real and prasiolite will inspire you to appreciate yourself and your true talents.

OTHER CRYSTALS WITH SIMILAR PROPERTIES: emerald, labradorite, malachite, moonstone

Sunstone

TO RADIATE LOVE

When you're feeling happy and want to express joy from every pore, to radiate the glory of true love, take the warm yellow sunstone. Take it not only to enhance your glow but to regain personal power and strength as you accept the end of self-sabotage, replacing it with the power of self-worth. Sunstone will burn through the delusion of self-doubt – the lies you tell yourself – so you glow as if you've been on a lifelong vacation and people cannot help but comment on the difference in your shine.

OTHER CRYSTALS WITH SIMILAR PROPERTIES: aventurine, citrine, golden healer quartz, moonstone, rose quartz, tiger's eye

We are mirrors; we reflect our beliefs back into the world. We are also magnets and what we believe, we attract – our energy works like the claw hand on the crane grabber in the games at the fair, reaching out to what it is we desire. Often our desires and intentions are just a little out of sync because we don't feel worthy of them, so we undersell, undermine and undervalue ourselves. We can bring close our crystal tribe to realign that thinking, to connect to what it is we truly need instead of desperately grabbing at what we think we want.

CRYSTALS FOR ACHIEVING YOUR DREAMS AND GOALS

Moonstone

FOR PROTECTION AND BALANCE WHEN EXPLORING THE UNKNOWN

Often when we explore new territory, new thought patterns, new needs or desires, it can be scary. When you decide you want that new coat, you go out and you buy it because you deserve it; that is what you work hard for. So why not take that up a level, to the bigger things in life? You want the new house, the dream car, the promotion? Moonstone is the most peaceful of stones, seeking to shroud you in its calming protective energy, and to draw in and out of your life exactly what you need, when you need it – as the moon controls her tides – reducing the worries about having enough or being enough. Equally, it can be used when you are looking to ensure balance and health in all your relationships – romantic, professional, financial, or with yourself. Use moonstone to draw into your life those who seek to support you, and feel her love strengthening and guiding you in these ventures.

OTHER CRYSTALS WITH SIMILAR PROPERTIES: celestite, chrysoprase, labradorite, selenite

Lapis Lazuli

FOR MAKING IT REAL

What we speak, we ultimately become. We use our words, our mouths, to speak our desires into existence. This is one of the most powerful forms of manifestation. When we say, 'I am magic, I am lucky', we become these things, just as when we say, 'I am worthless, I am unlikable', we retreat and carry those qualities into our day. Consider the beautiful blue lapis lazuli as the harmonizer of our thoughts. Lean into her to promote the most positive messages. Draw this crystal in when looking for an honest, fair and truly constructive conversation – be it with another being or with your guides in the sky.

OTHER CRYSTALS WITH SIMILAR PROPERTIES: angelite, apatite, blue lace agate

Iolite

FOR PERSPECTIVE AND FREEDOM TO CREATE A POWERFUL HERE AND NOW

Seeing is believing. How we 'see' life, people and situations adds color and shape to our existence. If you like someone, you see all their finest qualities; if you fall out with that same person, the list of negative things about them all of a sudden multiplies tenfold. There is great magic in seeing both sides of the coin, in being able to detach and separate out your

own truths and those of others. Even if you don't completely agree, taking a step back to reflect is powerful. How we visualize life is a powerful catalyst for bringing that life into being. Iolite is a truly precious crystal: not only will it gently cleanse and enable your spiritual sight to perceive things, situations and people as they truly are, it will also help you make peace – forgiving, forgetting and holding those same situations and people in a warm and loving glow. Used in manifestation exercises, iolite can free your mind from worry, taking the weight off and allowing your imagination to fly as freely as when you were a child.

OTHER CRYSTALS WITH SIMILAR PROPERTIES: amethyst, aventurine, howlite, lapis lazuli

Emerald
FOR STRENGTHENING YOUR FOUNDATIONS AND RELATIONSHIPS

Often we can find ourselves spinning multiple plates – thoughts, emotions, events, worries. It can be exhausting trying to predict which one is going to drop first. Perspective here is vital, as is patience. It's important that we grow daily, not just upwards but into our roots, so that when the storms of life blow in seemingly from nowhere, we know ourselves to be securely attached to our foundations. Emerald is a teacher, eager to show you how. The gateway to bliss (even during life's stormier moments) can be uncovered by the gentle, green emerald and it is one to be explored with patience. Promoting unity and stability in your relationships – with yourself, with a partner, with a parent – emerald will work with you tirelessly to secure you at your roots so that you can yield reliable, trusting relationships, and have faith in life delivering to you unified, stable and unconditional love.

OTHER CRYSTALS WITH SIMILAR PROPERTIES: aventurine, apache tear, moss agate, tiger's eye, stromalite

Angelite
TO GET YOURSELF CONNECTED

To have relationships means to connect and in this beautiful, crazy age of technology, it's all too easy to reach out into life through your phone or through your computer. Consequently, there is always something missing from what we are seeking there. Call in the feathered touch of angelite to remind you of your connections to people and life at a human level, to unblock your energy path, to raise your awareness and to allow you to walk through life with an open heart, an outstretched hand and at a tranquil and balanced pace.

OTHER CRYSTALS WITH SIMILAR PROPERTIES: amethyst, celestite, lapis lazuli, labradorite

Spessartine

TO TAKE WHAT YOU NEED

In order to receive, we must drop the guilt of asking and balance it with our desire to give. How many times have you said to yourself, 'I wish I'd asked for that'? How many missed opportunities have flown by because you've been left tongue-tied? Spessartine will help you balance your scales, encouraging you to ask and take what you need free of guilt, pushing you gently into a space of rational thinking so that you can express yourself without fear. It'll also promote your willingness to help others. Spessartine will sit with you during times of darkness and light the way as it lifts you during those blue days. Know what you want but too scared to ask for it? Not any more.

OTHER CRYSTALS WITH SIMILAR PROPERTIES: aventurine, moldavite, opal, pyrite

How we start our day is vital. As the sun rises, the curtains draw back on the play of life. How exciting, to be alive in a day that's never been experienced before – not by anyone. It's an adventure and we so often forget to be grateful for it. Guess what? How you shape your day is all down to you. You are the director of your play, the lead actor, the costume and set designer. Sure, your castmates are a little out of your control, but if you choose your mood and choose it wisely, life and the cast and crew will vibe right back with you. And if they don't? Just grab your crystal, yell, 'Scene change', and move on.

CRYSTALS FOR STARTING THE DAY RIGHT

Amazonite

FOR MAKING LIFE YOUR PLAYGROUND

Amazonite is one of my all-time favorite crystals and one I love to wake up to, for Amazonite promotes the sense that the world is our playground. It reminds us what it means to be 'whole' and connected to so much more than ourselves and our personal attachments. Seek out this beautiful lace-patterned green and white crystal to feel a sense of completeness before you leave the house. Eradicate that sense of there being something missing, freeing you up for play and excitement. Our bodies may grow up, but there is always time for play with our inner child, making the day fun, dancing into it.

OTHER CRYSTALS WITH SIMILAR PROPERTIES: aventurine, red calcite, rose quartz, tiger's eye

Red Calcite

FOR A CAFFEINE HIT

We'd all like to jump out of bed but sometimes we need an extra kick to get us going. That's why we drink coffee, and crave sugar, right? It gives us a kick. How many of us believe we cannot start our day without one of these guilty pleasures? I'm putting my hand up. So why not turn to a guilt-free, harm-free kick? Red calcite is your morning-coffee hit, energizing us in the belly, with a buzz that reminds us to go out and take hold of life. It's a really powerful stone when we want to restore our mojo, vitality and lust for life.

OTHER CRYSTALS WITH SIMILAR PROPERTIES: citrine, diamond, sunstone

Celestite
FOR WALKING CAREFREE, HEAD HELD HIGH

We spend so much time shuffling into our day, with our noses practically touching our toes as our minds hit our desks long before we've arrived at our place of work. Getting through our commute unscathed, unseen, undisturbed, is a huge tick on the checklist – but why? Shouldn't life be about standing tall and saying, 'Here I am'? If you want to feel happy all the time, to actively enjoy the journey into work, get celestite close to your skin. Celestite guides and develops intuition. She will inspire you to walk with your heart and your senses fully alert, creating the most magical days as you become aware of life pointing you in the right direction. Play with her; she will lead you peacefully through your day!

OTHER CRYSTALS WITH SIMILAR PROPERTIES: aventurine, opal, smoky quartz

Aquamarine
TO SHAKE IT OFF

Sometimes we've had a bad day and we cannot shake it off. Sometimes someone else has had a bad day and they drown us in their negative vibes. Let's be realistic: these things often take time to let go their grip on us, so why not try to hasten the process along by inviting aquamarine to dance energetically over you, to shield you, to provide you with the courage you feel you've lost, to enable you to express harmony when all you can hear is discord? Allow her to help you feel compassion and sensitivity with others when life may not be so kind or forgiving. A beautiful crystal for allowing your sensitivities to transform over time into pure strength.

OTHER CRYSTALS WITH SIMILAR PROPERTIES: amber, aragonite, bloodstone, hematite

Diamond
FOR HOLDING ONTO A GOOD VIBE

Sometimes you wake up and your personal frequency is set exactly right; you know every song on the radio is your groove. When you have a great mood and you want to keep a tight hold of it, turn to diamond – think of her as your hairspray for life! Her precious cut purifies and cleanses your energy. Use when you're feeling strong, or relaxed, or excited, or positive – and want the feeling to last. Diamond is a true best friend for more than just her sparkle. (However, I would not recommend always sleeping in diamonds as her heightened buzz over prolonged periods has been known to cause restless sleep or insomnia.)

OTHER CRYSTALS WITH SIMILAR PROPERTIES: angelite, turquoise

Amber

FOR DUSTING YOURSELF DOWN

We need to leave yesterday where it is, in the past, and face today. Perhaps you have an energy hangover from the day before and need to clear the dust away. Perhaps you need a little protection going into a day where things have been left unresolved – perhaps an argument is still up in the air or you didn't get as much done as you'd planned – but you are determined not to let it hold you back. Use amber as a negativity duster and allow Lady Luck to replace whatever is stopping you from seeing things clearly, with some magical, heart-centered, good fortune. Think of amber as the light in your lighthouse, calling in all life's – as yet unseen – luck.

OTHER CRYSTALS WITH SIMILAR PROPERTIES: amethyst, aquamarine, black tourmaline

Opal
FOR FIXING YOUR CROWN

Opal is the queen of inspiration, especially when you're planning to make changes within yourself and more broadly in your life. Allow opal to fill you with a sense of hope and inner peace, enhancing your memory and kickstarting your imagination. Use on a cloudy-minded day to cut through to clarity and find comfort in your own light. Opal will help you glide through your day, reminding you to hold your chin up so that your crown doesn't slip.

OTHER CRYSTALS WITH SIMILAR PROPERTIES: amethyst, blue lace agate, celestite

We can underestimate the power of ending the day well. We jump into bed and bury ourselves under the covers in an attempt to cancel out the day we've just had. How many times have you moaned, 'Ugh, I wish today was over'? But it's important to slow ourselves and our energies right down, and use the end of the day to count our blessings and turn to reflection. It's essential for us to calm down after a day of mania, overexcitement and stress. Use your crystals like your comforter – your cuddly toy – that you secretly hug at night. This is the time to surrender fully to the night.

CRYSTALS FOR ENDING THE DAY RIGHT

Amethyst

FOR PLUGGING YOURSELF IN FOR AN OVERNIGHT CHARGE

Amethyst is one of our staple go-to stones. It is most effective for resting and transitioning into a deep, dreamy sleep. The enriching and vibrant amethyst allows us to delicately lift the veil between the physical world and the world in the skies above us, channelling our emotions into a bridge to the 'beyond', helping us to let our minds truly rest. I would recommend holding amethyst for a good hour before going to bed, as you start to zone out in order to zone in, letting your mind drift away from the things you wish you'd done differently, the conversations you wish you'd had or not had, and counting your blessings for the ultimate dreamy sleep.

OTHER CRYSTALS WITH SIMILAR PROPERTIES: aragonite, howlite, moonstone, selenite

Howlite
FOR STILLING THE MIND

Howlite should be embraced by night to still your mind. A natural sponge for emotional turbulence, sweet howlite – green, white or blue – will rock you calmly to sleep even during the wildest of days, while also working in your zen and dreamlike state to strengthen your memory. Ask howlite to set your mental frequency to peace, to the deep rest of a calm heart and tranquil thoughts.

OTHER CRYSTALS WITH SIMILAR PROPERTIES: apatite, clear quartz, amethyst

Aragonite
FOR A HEALING SLEEP

Sometimes the day can leave us sky high or off center for both 'good' and 'bad' reasons. Aragonite is a crystal of the earth; it is a grounding healer. Work with aragonite to feel comfortable in your skin, in your surroundings, to center you when you feel spun out, and to alleviate the tensions of the day in a warm and calming manner.

OTHER CRYSTALS WITH SIMILAR PROPERTIES: amethyst, labradorite, orange calcite, golden healer quartz

Selenite

FOR SELF-REFLECTION

At the end of the day it's important to review and check in on progress made. Use selenite to bookend your days: allow her to stabilize you and raise peace from the deep wells within you. Selenite is your trusted friend when you need to clear confusion from within yourself or from a difficult situation.

OTHER CRYSTALS WITH SIMILAR PROPERTIES: amethyst, labradorite, turquoise

Sapphire

FOR MANIFESTING A BRIGHTER TOMORROW

To become like the night owl and call in your inner wisdom, take a hold of sapphire and free yourself from your mental tensions, calm your mind, center your soul and move into a state of magnetisation and manifestation. Surrender to sapphire and allow your dreams to do the work of creating the life you are crafting on your mental mood board.

OTHER CRYSTALS WITH SIMILAR PROPERTIES: diamond, howlite, moonstone, sunstone

Apatite

FOR MASSAGING THE MIND

To wake up with a bounce, we need to find some balance overnight: apatite will take care of you both mentally and physically. Call on apatite – your mind masseuse – when you've had an over-stimulating day. Perhaps you've hit the gym late and are still feeling pumped, or you've had two more than your usual three coffees, or you've laughed the night away with friends. Steadily restore your balance without losing all the good vibes you've generated.

OTHER CRYSTALS WITH SIMILAR PROPERTIES: amethyst, black tourmaline, howlite, jade

Golden Healer Quartz

FOR OPENING YOUR HEART

Part of the quartz family, the golden healer is a superstar stone, promoting healing on all levels – physical, metaphysical, emotional. You name it, she has you covered. Whatever the focus, the crisis, the quandary, the emotion or the desire, ask golden healer to seek for what you need, while holding you in a heavenly, loving and heart-opening state.

OTHER CRYSTALS WITH SIMILAR PROPERTIES: amethyst, aventurine, clear quartz, moss agate, peridot

Barite

FOR BIG DREAMING

Barite is a stone of the soul. Finish your day feeling right by calling on this crystal for a deeply restful vibe. For an all-time sleep high, barite is my go-to crystal of choice. On those mornings when you wake and know you've had a big dream, but you cannot for the life of you remember what it was, call in barite to enhance dream recall so that you can apply the secrets your dreams reveal to your waking day.

OTHER CRYSTALS WITH SIMILAR PROPERTIES: amethyst, howlite, labradorite

Different ways of buying require different approaches. Trying before you buy is incredibly important: a face-to-face meeting to shake hands with your crystal in store is my preferred style of purchase. However, we shouldn't rule out online stores, because there are some really fantastic ones. We just need to change and develop our approach in the selection process.

This can be somewhat intimidating or overwhelming if you allow your ego to slide in. Remember your *intuition* is the key, your energy, your call. You may already have the crystal of your choice in mind, or you may have an idea of what you want to work on with a crystal, and are applying a more intuitive approach to the selection.

WHERE TO PURCHASE YOUR CRYSTALS

Let's go shopping

Allow your mind and heart to be open; set your intention to what exactly it is you need; ask that it appear, that it be shown to you. Take time to explore the store. Remember the choice is yours and it should be a fun experience. You will often find the smaller tumble stones are all hanging out together in one pot, whereas the wands and the more expensive crystals are locked behind a glass door. Don't just go for what's on top or in view or easiest to get to. Move the pieces to see what attracts your eye. Select a few, pick them up and feel them; place them in your hand, close your eyes … If you're not comfortable with that, look up and away from your hand and focus on your breathing, move back to your intention, 'which piece is right is right for me, right now'. They will start to call back, to tickle or prickle or buzz; they will feel hot or cold. Whichever way a crystal calls to you will feel right. That is *your* crystal; that's you *connecting*.

If you are choosing for a friend, a loved one, all that needs to be changed is the intention: 'What does Becky need right now?'; 'What's the perfect gift for Mom or Maya?'; 'What's calling for Andy?' Again, *play* with it. Walk around the shop, but this time you're walking on behalf of someone else – so hold them in your heart and mind.

It's the same with the online stores, but we just have to get clever with our feelings, our intuition. See it as a challenge, and a fun one. As we know with online dating and social media, what looks pretty in the picture is possibly not an exact representation of what's going to land on our doorstep. So scan the store, with not only the intention of 'what is right for me' as before, but also 'please allow the perfect piece to be delivered to me'. Trust is key here: trust in your intuition, turn the volume up and drown out the self-doubt.

With each and every type of store, read the reviews and ask questions. Where do they source their crystals from? It's important they're ethically and fairly traded. And if they don't know, then I'd say that's a loud no-go.

PAY FAIR

For the smaller tumble stones, you will be looking at paying upwards of $3. The palm stones and wands will be at a starting price of $7 to $11.

The rarity of the stone will of course affect the price. For larger pieces, I would expect to be charged by weight. If not, ask how the value is arrived at. Some stores will add on a whopping mark-up, so if it *feels* off, question and challenge it.

STORES

I love London's witching quarter, Covent Garden. My favorite store of choice – because of its authenticity – is The Astrology Store on Neal Street, run by Barry and the gang. It is quite like stepping into another beautiful and bewitching world (www.londonastrology.com).

Mysteries is literally just down the road and is also high on my list of go-to stores (www.mysteries.co.uk).

Different crystal stores have very different vibes and, as ever, what may be right for one person is not right for all – so explore them all.

Camden market is awesome for crystal jewellery, as is Monica Vinader (www.monicavinader.co.uk) – of whom I am a big devotee, especially of her rings – they're perfectly picked, perfectly set – and when you've set your intention to them – you won't just be glistening, you will be rocking!

ONLINE

I am a huge fan of The Crystal Cactus and The Beautiful Dot and also of using Amazon and Etsy!

The first two I actually discovered through social media and word of mouth – there is a huge cluster of crystal promoters and suppliers becoming ever more present online. It's super cool that the community is developing this way

– it's positive vibration amplification at its finest – but, as with the stores and the crystals themselves, go looking into their store window (however this is situated) and call to your heart and belly and ask if that feels right for you. And then? Then you explore like you would when trying a new hairdresser or looking to go get a first-time piercing – ask does this feel like the place for me? Look around, ask the questions, read the reviews and the returns policy, play with your senses and trust that you'll be smart.

Review the further resources at the end of the book for more of my top picks both in person and online, including a selection of US and Canada based Stores for my readers there.

Cut some shapes

We know that there is a multitude of crystals with a multitude of uses, but there is also a multitude of formations they can take. Each shape transforms the crystal into something that not only looks different but projects its energy in a different way.

POINTS

Crystal points can be natural or artificial. They occur at their most powerful – I believe – in their natural form, when they've been separated out from a larger bed of crystals. They are superb for meditation and for the reduction of an ailment or emotion. How? By using the tiny point – facing towards your body to direct new energies inward and turning the point away to direct energies outward. Simple.

CLUSTERS

Clusters are multiple points of crystal heads – think of all the spikes on a hedgehog's back and how they work both together and independently. Clusters are to crystals as speaker systems are to sound: they are great amplifiers and radiators of energy, and are also great for cleansing rooms.

BALLS

Traditionally these were used by seers to foretell the future and they've been favored by psychics for years – but don't let the stereotype deter you from using or exploring crystal balls. Not only are they used to heighten intuitive abilities because they act as windows to the future and to the past, but they work much like a perfume diffuser, emitting energy in the most balanced state.

PYRAMIDS

Pyramids are great for refreshing your energies and can be used to move energy through the large base into the tiny yet laser-sharp point, either into or away from you.

EGGS

Eggs are super-duper soothing stones. They're nature's stress balls. Massage them in your hands to relieve tension or to refocus the mind, or use your crystal of choice shaped into an egg to massage your chakra points (see p.160), to diffuse anxiety or other emotional blockages on our path towards happiness.

WANDS

Yes, you've seen them in movies. You recognise the moment when the wizard flicks the wand to move the intention – or spell – into existence. Well, this is exactly what they are used for in crystal form. The crystal wand focuses the energy on its own power, the energy of your mind and of the universe and radiates it out through the wand's tip and amplifies it. Abracadabra!

GEODES

Not only are geodes aesthetically most pleasing to the eye, they are masters at moving and amplifying energy with incredible and powerful force. They neutralize and balance – perfect for use in the home.

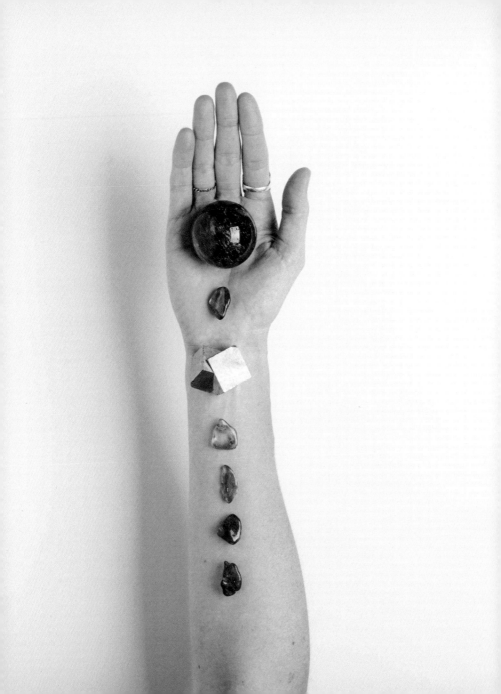

Crystal quality

A damaged crystal doesn't mean it's destined for the trash. As with human beings, there is often perfection to be found in imperfection. Some of my most treasured pieces have taken very different shapes from the ones they had when I first bought them. We should never judge a book by its cover, and that holds good for other things too. For me the cracks and the quirks in the crystal are often the most wonderful things about them: the chips allow for a differing vibration, a different way to explore their depths. One thing I would like you to think about is that when they break – if you drop them and they smash into two or more pieces – you've not made a massive life fail, you've actually created more surfaces for love, for energy; you've widened the platform. A smashed crystal is very different from a smashed mirror: allow the chinks, the seeming deformities of the piece to entice you.

Just like us, crystals need to maintain a certain level of cleanliness. When we have worn our clothes, we wash them to keep them fresh. We wash our hair to keep it clean and shiny when it's been exposed to everyday pollution. And we wash ourselves to wash away the day or just to wake up and refresh ourselves. It's important we keep up a cleansing routine with our crystals, because in the same way that our minds or the batteries in our phones or computers can be charged to full power, so can these wondrous healers.

Remember that these beauties, while they are charging and aligning our vibe, are also absorbing and transmuting negative or low-vibing energies. They need to reset and realign to restore their soft and gentle flow.

HOW TO
CLEANSE
YOUR
CRYSTALS

Ways to cleanse and charge

WATER PURIFICATION

Cold or cool water is as refreshing to the crystal as it is to our skin. Imagine standing and moving under a waterfall – it's invigorating. You might like to turn on the tap and rinse the crystals through in your hands – or you might prefer to run them a bath in your sink or in a bowl of water and allow them to soak as you would yourself in a bath or in the sea.

You do not need any soaps or detergents. You can, however, add Himalayan salts to a soak for that extra cleanse. Allow your crystals to dry on a natural fabric in daylight or by the light of the moon. I would use moonlight for those crystals that are more housebound and starting to gather a little dust internally as well as externally.

It is important to note that some crystals, such as selenite, should not be placed in water as they will dissolve.

SUN SHOWERS

Masterful sunlight fuels the world; it fuels our very existence – and for crystals it is no different. Sunlight moves through and warms even the hardest of materials. I would suggest, for extra effect, showering or bathing your crystals and then moving them outside not only to cleanse them but to allow them to be fuelled by the sun's gentle rays. If you do not have access to outdoor space, the rays of the sun penetrating through a window are equally powerful. Observe how the crystals twinkle after being kissed by the sun.

MOON BATHS

Cleansing crystals at a full moon is always my preference. It's pure magic how Mama Moon removes the toxins from your charms and at the same time from yourself. It also offers you a regular cleansing cycle as she graces us in totality every lunar month without fail – even when you can't see her behind the clouds, you can feel her presence. She has an incredibly special connection with crystals – as she does with all nature. Shower or soak your crystals in water and then lay them outside or on the windowsill to allow the moon to bathe them.

CANDLE CHARGE

As always when working with fire, you need to take care. This is my quick-fix charge – think of it like plugging in your phone to top up the battery. If I've had a 'toxic' day or I've been exposed to some unwanted or unexpected bad vibes, I will always cross my crystal through the very tip of a candle flame. You don't need to hold it too close for the heat to burn off the bad energy. Pass it through once or twice and then place it on a natural surface, cloth, sand, soil or Himalayan salts, to ground it and to allow it to settle and soak in the recharge.

SMUDGING IT OUT

Smudge sticks are fantastic – white sage would be my go-to here. Light the smudge stick as instructed on the packaging and allow the smoke to pass gently over your crystal collection. The smoke from the smudge stick will track down the negativity – much like a sniffer dog trained to perfection – and cancel it.

ENERGY HEALING

Energy healing is wondrous. It's used on our bodies to reorient the spirit and to best allow the body to heal itself. If you are interested in energy work such as reiki, you can take your crystal to sessions to recharge at the same time as you do.

OTHER TIMES TO CLEANSE YOUR CRYSTALS

You might sense a need to cleanse your crystals in addition to your regular cleansing routine, or when a crystal feels 'full'.

When a crystal first arrives home from the store, remember that it has passed through many hands before reaching yours and every fingerprint leaves an energetic mark – so cleanse before use.

Much as we love our family and friends, they do tend to think they have an open invitation to investigate our things. If you don't want to seem rude by asking them not to touch, allow them to explore – it's cool that they're as intrigued as you are – but be sure to cleanse your crystals afterwards.

We all have different ways of working. We all have different heightened senses – what it is for me to see may be for you to feel. This is why it is so important not only to explore the crystals themselves but also to explore how you communicate with them. How you talk to a friend may not be how you talk to a teacher; how you talk to a personal trainer is not how you would talk to your doctor. We might have to adapt a little of ourselves, and not give up too readily.

CRYSTAL MEDITATION AND CHAKRAS

You may be well practiced in meditation – that is cool. You may think you have no clue nor time to even begin to explore the possibilities of meditation. Well, the good news is, we all breathe! If we strip meditation right, *right* back to its bare bones, it's essentially focus, coupled with breathing beautifully – that's all you need to begin.

Take your crystals of choice. If you don't know which those are, remember to ask, 'What's my intention?' I would start with one crystal in your palm and then over time take one in each hand at the start of your practice.

As you breathe, focus your attention on the crystals lying gently in the center of your hands (there are chakra points here – read more about this in the next section). You can place your hands gently on your knees as you sit in whatever way is comfortable for you – on a chair, on the floor, in full lotus or with your legs stretched out wide – or, if you prefer, you can be lying down with your body supported by the ground or a bed. Now simply count your breathing. In and out for a count of four; in and out for five; in and out all the way up to ten. You will start to become aware of your hands, of the weight of the crystal; feel its magic start to buzz. Your mind will start to dispel it – but have the faith and the heart to trust it.

VERBAL COMMUNICATION

If meditation is not your thing, perhaps you're more of a verbal communicator. To you I would say hold your crystals and talk to them, feel them. We work best with direction and so do the crystals. If you have a specific intention to set, say it out loud.

ATTUNING YOUR CRYSTALS

You can use a crystal therapist or an energy healer to do this for you, but when this isn't an option or you would rather do this yourself, it is possible to use the power of your own intention. Decide what it is you wish the crystal to aid you with or enhance within you. For example, if I wanted to see my true worth, I would use my trusted labradorite (see p. 78), holding it in my hand during meditation or in a quiet space and set my attention with its assistance: 'Please help me see my soul's purpose, my pure real beauty, my worth. Allow it to shine through all the obstacles that currently seek to block it.'

Working with your chakras

WHAT ARE CHAKRAS?

In short – and this is really short because they are such wonderfully beautiful and complex parts of our make-up – chakras are power points of energy on the surface of our body. Try to visualize these points spinning like wheels or vortexes, pulling the outer or 'universal' energies to the core of our innermost self, in order to align, balance and ease the physical, metaphysical and mental systems in and around the body. And where do the crystals come into play here? Well, they act as magnifying glasses and magnets to enhance energies into these points and deeper into our being.

Like our crystals – like us – each chakra has its own vibrational frequency, and each one governs a specific function of the human body.

There are seven 'key' chakra points that run along and through you, top to tail – these are the focus of our crystal chakra meditation. But we have many more chakra points to be explored – for example on our hands and faces. This is why we can stimulate love and a healthy glow by rubbing rose quartz on to our faces or why we feel the crystals hum as they lie still in our palms. These vortexes, these energy wheels, these points, run right through you. The diagram overleaf may lead you to believe they are flat and simply run up the front of the body, but they run right through front to back and back to front. Let your mind visualise this in 3D.

HEALING WITH CRYSTALS

In a healing session, crystals are laid along the key chakra line of the body to aid in balancing our energy field. We also have chakra/energy points in our hands and I find these points, as well as the third eye – the point between our eyebrows – most effective when I am starting therapy with a beginner. Find out how to work your chakras in the following section.

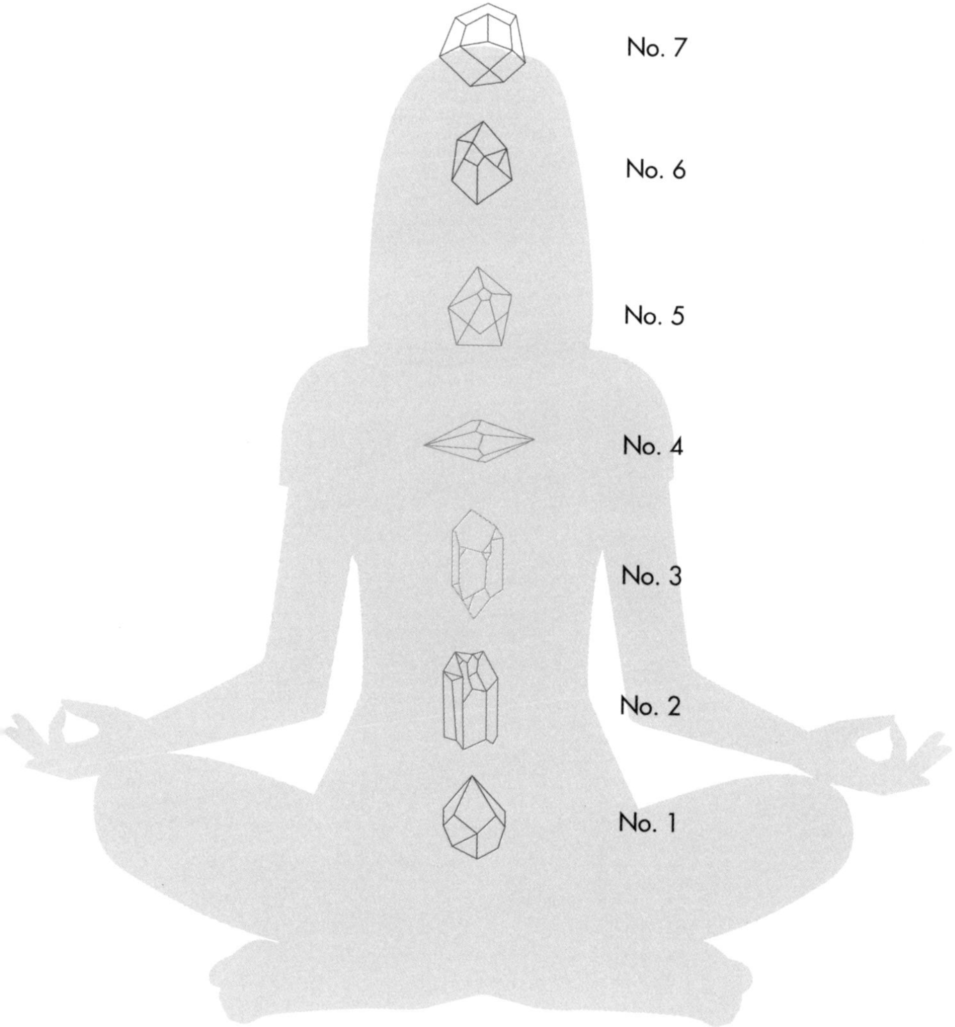

No. 7

No. 6

No. 5

No. 4

No. 3

No. 2

No. 1

CHAKRA NO. 7

NAME: Crown

CRYSTALS: Amethyst

COLOR: Violet

INTENTION: I understand

PROMOTES AND BALANCES:
Intuitive development, thinking, understanding

CHAKRA NO. 6

NAME: Third Eye

CRYSTALS: Iolite

COLOR: Indigo

INTENTION: I see

PROMOTES AND BALANCES:
Perception, spiritual sight

CHAKRA NO. 5

NAME: Throat

CRYSTALS: Blue lace agate

COLOR: Bright blue

INTENTION: I speak

PROMOTES AND BALANCES:
Communication, creativity

CHAKRA NO. 4

NAME: Heart

CRYSTALS: Rose quartz/peridot

COLOR: Green

INTENTION: I love

PROMOTES AND BALANCES:
Love, compassion, affection, self-acceptance

CHAKRA NO. 3

NAME: Solar plexus

CRYSTALS: Citrine, amber

COLOR: Yellow

INTENTION: I do

PROMOTES AND BALANCES:
Will power, tension release, emotional calming

CHAKRA NO. 2

NAME: Sacral

CRYSTALS: Carnelian

COLOR: Orange

INTENTION: I feel

PROMOTES AND BALANCES: Power, energizing, vitality, sexuality, pleasure

CHAKRA NO. 1

NAME: Base

CRYSTALS: Ruby, onyx, obsidian

COLOR: Red

INTENTION: I am

PROMOTES AND BALANCES:
Grounding, overall health, stillness, stability

Chakra meditation

The good thing is you don't need to be a chakra expert to have try go at meditating a little more deeply with your energy centers and your crystals.

Use the diagram to find each chakra's focal point and the crystals recommended to work each one. If you're new to chakra meditation you might find it easier to hold the crystals in your hands against each chakra point, as opposed to placing them.

Meditation does not necessarily require closed eyes, though closing your eyes can help you to focus and open your mind.

During meditation or quiet repose place your crystal on the corresponding chakra, or if you would like to experience or transmute a more specific feeling – say, for example, a feeling of confidence – then meditate and place a tiger's eye at your sacrum to enhance the powers and effects; if you wish to feel more love, take rose quartz to the heart chakra; to enhance the power of communication, turquoise to your throat, etc.

Here are two types of chakra meditation to explore. If trying to meditate while reading is not your thing, you can download an audio chakra meditation. Keep the crystals aligned to your energy centers and listen to the guidance.

CHAIN-MEDITATION

Lying flat out, you can place the relevant crystal on the body or aligned by the body as directed above by the diagram.

Start by focusing on the breath, closing the eyes to soften vision and pulling your attention to the within.

Bring 'attention' (in your mind's eye) to the first chakra point, the base, and feel the gentle buzz of the crystal here. The base is the connection to earth. Ask for this to be shown to you in whichever way is best for you – the color we are taught is associated with it, a symbol, a word or a feeling.

Then focus on the chakra itself and its associated crystal – however it is shown to you. Visualize this 'wheel', the energy spinning, watching the direction of its flow, breathing into the light, the shape, the space, just observing, trusting. Watch as your breath expands the light, the brightness of the chakra, and enhances the buzz or pulsation, moving from the crystal. (This is the cleansing – the brighter, the more vivid, the better. Your mind may try to tell you it is not working but it is.)

Then start to visualize the energy at the chakra spinning in a clockwise direction. (To spin clockwise is to be in balance. When we spin counter-clockwise our energy is in 'negative form'.) Feel its warmth or coolness as well as the crystal's. Remember, we are all different: this is about what resonates with you; it's not about being right or wrong. Every breath sent with the intention of expanding and cleansing is a powerful source. Allow the crystal to buzz and pulse as you have done before; allow it to magnify and amplify the positive promotion of positive energies to these points.

Move upwards and repeat at each point. Work your way up and up to chakra 7, the crown. There is no rush to move through this process. Each chakra, each point, is individual, and some will require more love on different days.

As you reach 7th heaven – your crown chakra – allow yourself in your mind's eye to step back and witness your whole body. Scan the whole body, feel the crystals. Does everything feel as if it is open and aligned? Are you positively buzzing? Breathe into every point and then allow your breath to move from the crown chakra right through to the base and back up again; allow each crystal to be a marker for these points. This feels delicious as it is here that you will find your flow.

Remember: trust your gut. You will know intuitively where you need to spend more time. You will observe which space, which point is opening more quickly, expanding with ease, and which has more resistance; how each point 'feels' to you or moves you. This is where you resume work next time. It's important to observe how you feel, each time you meditate you will witness just how different you are each day, each week, each month. This is how you 'measure' your results.

FOCUSING ON A PARTICULAR VIBE

An alternative way to work with your chakras, start by focusing on what you really want to concentrate your efforts on and select the crystal with the specific effects you wish to transpire. Let's take, for example, expanding your voice. Here we would need to turn to our throat chakra and a turquoise crystal.

Begin as before but focus your attention directly on your throat; the crystal this time should be positioned and held at your energy center, your chakra with your hand.

With your mind's eye observing and focusing on the throat – the space just outside your body rather than your tonsils – start to focus on the feel of your crystal, the buzz and tickle of your crystal of choice, and visualize the associated chakra color – in the case of the throat, the color blue. Visualise the energy wheel spinning and enlarging and trust the crystal's connection with it. With every breath, it expands.

CONNECTING WITH YOUR LIFE FORCE

Working with chakras and with crystals, you are focusing on a physical and metaphysical level on a connection with your life force. In meditation we often use our practice to free our thoughts, to allow for and make space for us to just be, steadying the mind and letting the benefits resonate through the body. With a chakra crystal meditation, you are actively participating with your whole body while calling on nature's gems to enhance the effects, exploring your own layers and levels and that of the crystals but in a more healing way, witnessing the effects of thoughts and feelings and energy on the power that is you.

We are actively pulling in source energy and taking responsibility for our body and its internal needs – those beautiful networks within us that pressure of time often means we overlook. Working chakras works mind, body and spirit – rather than other forms of meditation, which allow us to work the mind only.

There have always been different ideas about improving our energy levels and making our environments more conducive to our work, rest and play. Crystals too can be used to create this magic. With all things of the earth, as with human beings, these things work so beautifully in unity.

CRYSTALS IN THE HOME, WORK AND WARDROBE

The healing home

No one knows your home better than you. And if you have a housemate or a partner, you each bring your own qualities into the home to create a balance of and for you both. If something doesn't 'feel' or 'look' as it should, you move it and you move it again until it's 'right'. You experiment and you explore. Then you add flowers for color and to reflect the mood and they change with the seasons. You have items in the living room you wish to share and you've items in your personal space – your bedroom or office desk – that are just for you. Crystals are just the same. They can bring that vibe into you; they magnetize it towards you; they can stand tall and vibrate specific energies for intentional outcomes in every part of you and your life: your home, your car, your office, your den, your family.

With all that in your thoughts, allow your home in your mind to become the embodiment of you: your rooms become your chakra points, your energy centers and your desks, corners and favorite spaces become powerful locations for home manifesting intentions and the promotion of your high vibes.

HOME COMFORTS

Want love in your life, every shade of love? Then allow the rose quartz, sunstone, peridot – or whichever of your newly found crystal set cheerlead for love – to run riot in the heart or hearts of your house – your bedroom, bathroom, living room. If your heart lies in the kitchen, that is *your* heart center in the home.

Perhaps your intention is to cleanse? And not just yourself. Then let's get amber – or the crystal community of negativity spongers – by the running water points so the 'bad' vibes wash down the plug drain with the remnants on your dinner plate or the germs on your hand.

You honestly could not ask for a better housemate than a crystal and it need not just be the one – it can be a cluster of crystals or even a crystal shrine; go as little or as large as you like. What is more, they can live and thrive anywhere; they don't have to be confined to your bedroom. Perhaps you place them by the windowsill to reflect the light and you can add others to the dark corners where you feel a lack of light. I have them everywhere. They are an extension of self, so they have a free rein over the house but it's here we turn back to talking to them, to asking them, to feeling them. Much like hanging a picture, or placing a table, ask yourself where do they look right. How does that feel?

As with kids, so with adults. I have been known to tuck a piece in my sister's sock drawer to throw a little sparkle her way when she was still in her 'this is not really my kind of thing' mindset. I knew she had to find her own way with it. With your friends, parents or partner, it's their choice, just as it is yours. If gifting a crystal right now doesn't feel right, then set the intention for it and pop it in a place that represents them – and allow it to vibe.

WORK HARD

At work, it's important that we keep ourselves aligned in our own energy and keep ourselves safe from the technological vibes, the people vibes, the other 'stuff' people carry into the everyday and that we cannot control. So keeping crystals on your desk (tiger's eye, quartz, hematite, jet) to reduce pollution is important. You need once again to set the intention here; you need to ask that the crystal or crystals protect you from the noise that isn't for you and you need to make sure you keep them as clean as the crystals you have at home. If you're not feeling ready to sprinkle them over your desk, that's fine – this is a personal practice – you could get creative and use your crystals as bookends. My dad is what I call 'a questionable fan', so I bought him a crystal paperweight. That worked for him. What works for you?

Let's look back to wanting to kick butt at work (see p. 55). Place a stellar piece of your chosen crystal in your office, on your desk, in your drawer. If you have a big meeting and want to vibe in luck and opportunity, then place a piece of ruby by your calendar to pull in that focused vibe. Everything and anything goes – just so long as it works for you!

ADORN YOURSELF

And why can't we all be kings and queens? Let's adorn ourselves – do ourselves the utmost justice and *sparkle*. In the day I wear them; as jewellery they adorn my every finger, my wrists. I even have a locket with little chippings of rose quartz to hang near my heart so I can call in and radiate that loving feeling at any point of the day. Jewellery is particularly powerful because it is skin on skin and the touch of a crystal intertwining with our own energy to promote the powers and the secrets they keep is wonderful. And if you're not in the mood for them? If you're not 'feeling' it today, listen to that intuition, that insight, and change the crystal. You can get creative here: you can buy necklaces that act as little cages for your favourite pieces, allowing you to change the crystal as you choose – how cool is that? If jewellery isn't your thing, pop the crystal in your purse or your pocket, wherever suits you. When you have intention, you have connection, so the crystal doesn't need to be in line of sight always to be effective. Crystals will work hard wherever you place them.

I sleep with my crystals, in my hand, under my pillow, on my bedside table. I pull in my friends to carry me to deep sleep. One day having a crystal in my bed might irritate me, so I place it on the side table. I carry them in my pockets, my purse and most often in my bra – there is something powerful about their touch against skin. On occasion walking with them in your hand down the street may not be the most convenient! Let's not stick to rules; let's let them guide us.

CREATING AN ATMOSPHERE

If you're looking to heighten a mood, turn to crystal candle-holders. They are magnificent and they magnify the intention. The most common crystal candle-holders are quartz but you can also buy selenite lights, where a light-bulb-sized shape has been perfectly carved within them for the ultimate mood lighting. If this feels a bit 'woo woo' to you and you'd rather opt for a more decorative display, there are other pieces to explore.

If you want to give your children the excitement of this exploration too – pop a crystal within sight of their cot. If they're starting to be more hands-on in their exploration of the everyday, then keep a piece out of harm's reach: tuck it in a drawer or a cupboard in their room too large or heavy for them to open yet.

And it doesn't stop there. We can bathe ourselves with the crystals for a cleanse – we can use water this time instead of the light to magnify the vibration. Place the non-soluble crystal in the bath while the water is running, as you would your bubble bath, and climb in for a crystal submersion.

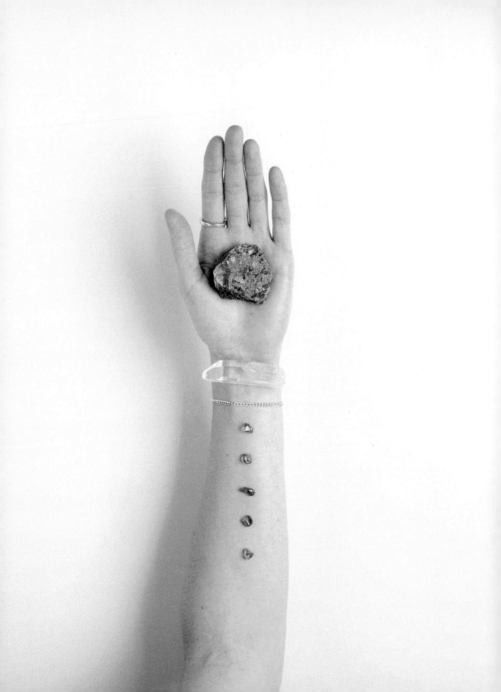

Energize your life

We can transform our lives when we take our crystals into our hands and into our hearts, working with their power to amplify our own and building a routine around them, a practice that suits us.

High vibing and powering up with crystals is so much more than a trend – it's a life movement and one that's here to stay. Taking the reins by changing and charging our lives is possible for all of us. With crystals – whether placed on our energy centers, sat next to our bedside or tucked into a back pocket – we can tap deeper into life and explore it more adventurously.

Further explorations in the world of vibrations

For more information on Emma Lucy, to book a session or to just ask a question – please visit www.youremmylou.com or get social @your_emmylou.

ENERGY HEALERS

Choosing an energy, crystal or reiki healer is as personal a process as picking the crystals. Here are a couple to start your exploration whom I am beyond blessed to recommend:

Alexandra Swann
alexandraswannreflexology.co.uk

Stephen Turoff
ministrymoe.org

Sound healing is powerful tool and the effect of sound on the body is definitely worth exploring – for balancing your chakras, or for soothing your soul and bones with the beautiful vibration of its healing, balancing and powerful tones.

Lisa Pauley
lisapauley.co.uk

Rosella Longinotti
rosella-creations.co.uk

If you need something more local to you and don't know where to find out – please ask me, or check out:

collegeofpsychicstudies.co.uk

buddhaonabicycle.com

triyoga.com

FURTHER READING ON ALL THINGS SPIRITUAL

Reading is powerful in itself. Picking what feels right for you from a selection of reference books is important if you are going to develop your own feelings in this area.

These have been some of my favorite go-to texts through my life so far. They are all widely available:

Rhonda Byrne, *The Magic*
Rebecca Campbell,
Light is the New Black
The Foundation of Inner Peace
A Course in Miracles
Judy Hall, *The Crystal Bible*
Louise L. Hay,
You Can Heal Your Life
Esther and Jerry Hicks,
Ask and it is Given
Jessica Jacobs,
Chakras for Beginners
Michael A. Singer,
The Untethered Soul,
The Journey Beyond Yourself
Dr Brian Weiss,
Many Lives, Many Masters
Oprah Winfrey,
What I Know For Sure

TO PURCHASE CRYSTALS IN STORE

I cannot recommend nor cheerlead Barry and the team at The Astrology Store in London loudly enough. They are fluent in crystals and I believe you get real bang for your buck with these guys. The store is an authentic adventure in itself. Please dive in and explore:

londonastrology.com

MY FAVES IN NORTH AMERICA AND CANADA

House of Intuition *Los Angeles*
The Crystal Shrine *Burbank*
Gem Heaven *Seattle*
Star Woman Crystals *Temple*
Nature's Treasures *Austin*
Labrynth Walking *Myrtle Beach*
Stick, Stone & Bone *New York*
Evolve *Crystal Lake*
The Rock Store *Toronto*

TO PURCHASE CRYSTALS ONLINE

ONLINE STOCKISTS TO EUROPE,
NORTH AMERICA, AUSTRALIA
AND NEW ZEALAND

wildeones.com
shamanscrystal.co.uk
holisticshop.co.uk
thecolourfuldotboutique.com
goldirocks.co

ETSY INTERNATIONAL STOCKISTS

etsy.com/uk/shop/BlissCrystals
etsy.com/uk/shop/AURAMORE

CRYSTAL AND SPIRITUAL COURSES

gatewayworkshops.co.uk/
spiritual_courses/listing

EVENTS AND FESTIVALS

Wanderlust Festival
USA/UK/Europe/Australia/
New Zealand
wanderlust.com

Mind Body and Spirit Festival
London and Birmingham
mindbodyspirit.co.uk

About the author

Emma Lucy Knowles is a clairvoyant and an intuitive, a hands-on crystal healer and meditation teacher. Emma Lucy has worked with crystals and energy for well over fifteen years, having started her exploration of crystals at the tender age of seven. She became fascinated, 'quite by chance', with how they looked and felt – long before she intuitively began to listen to them, discover their magic and explore fully the treasures they held. She suffered a bout of childhood depression as a result of heightened sensitivities and powerful, unexplained senses. She had difficulty learning how to become and understand herself and how to communicate in a world in which she was striving far too hard to be 'normal'. Subsequently, living a full life made of enriching experiences, Emma Lucy has set about transforming her pain into power, and then sharing this life's work as a powerful benefit for all. She works with a worldwide base of people, helping them to discover and explore how to overcome and their own pain and transmute this – in their own way, in their own time – into heartfelt success. She has used her own life, her own experience, the power of energy and the power of crystals, to gather and guide a powerful crowd of souls that she lovingly calls 'The Overcomers'.

Index of crystals

Page numbers in *italics* refer to images so that you can identify all the crystals in this book. Page numbers in **bold** refer to the detailed description of a crystal's healing properties.

Index

Index of healing properties

Index

To Team Knowles – THANK YOU x 1000. Without your love, challenge and support I would have never striven as hard to become truly myself. To the great architect in the sky guiding us, to the crystals and the earth gently holding us and to those souls who make this world turn lovingly around me, you know who you are. TSD, Lucie Cave, Chocolate Button, The Ash OP, OG, my Bauer buddies, all those who have found me and bravely committed to the unknown by putting their faith in me and the skies above us – I am truly BLESSED.

This book is dedicated to the loving memory of Paula Bonner, Christopher Boyes, Tom Beard – my earth angels in flight who help guide me daily in spiritual sight.

STERLING ETHOS
New York

An Imprint of Sterling Publishing Co., Inc.
1166 Avenue of the Americas
New York, NY 10036

STERLING ETHOS and the distinctive Sterling Ethos logo are registered trademarks of Sterling Publishing Co., Inc.

Text © 2018 Emma Lucy Knowles
Photographs © 2018 Stephanie McLeod

First published in the United Kingdom by Pop Press in 2018
ISBN 978-1-4549-3286-4

Distributed in Canada by Sterling Publishing Co., Inc.
c/o Canadian Manda Group,
664 Annette Street
Toronto, Ontario M6S 2C8, Canada

For information about custom editions, special sales, and premium and corporate purchases, please contact Sterling Special Sales at 800-805-5489 or specialsales@sterlingpublishing.com.

Manufactured in China

10 9 8 7 6 5 4 3 2 1

sterlingpublishing.com

We'd also like to thank Barry and The Astrology Store for generously lending us their amazing collection of crystals for the shoot.